THE ULTIMATE GUIDE TO JOURNALING

HANNAH BRAIME

INDIVIDUATE PRESS

Individuate Press

Copyeditor: Denise Barker

Cover design: Will Moyer

CONTENTS

INTRODUCTION

Journal writing offers several wonderful opportunities. It offers him a chance to express the full and honest truth of his process with no degree of external judgment—and no pollution of an external reward. It allows him to expand and explore his consciousness in a safe and protected environment, and piece together the truths of his history at a pace entirely his own. No one from outside can push him, because his motivation, if it is to last over the long haul, must come from within.
—*Daniel Mackler*, Toward Truth

Welcome to *The Ultimate Guide to Journaling* and thank you for reading this book. I hope it will inspire your creativity, help you get to know yourself on a deeper level, and be an enjoyable read. Whether you have journaled for years or have picked up this book out of curiosity, in the following pages you'll find the tools and exercises you need to help you make the most out of pen and paper.

If I was going to label myself, it would be as an introvert, and I've always felt more comfortable writing than speaking. Writing helps me get my thoughts in order; it helps me explore feelings and beliefs; and it opens up worlds for me that I wouldn't otherwise see. I kept my first proper diary when I was around nine or ten. Since then, I have spent a substantial amount of time journaling in one way or another with words, pictures, and even musical compositions.

My relationship with journaling has changed a lot. At times, I have hated everything I wrote; at others, it's been a compulsion. Today I love journaling. I love experimenting with the way I journal, as well as exploring different methods of communicating with and expressing myself. Most of all, I love looking back and seeing how my journaling, my self-knowledge, and my thought patterns have evolved.

The Idea behind The Ultimate Guide to Journaling

I wrote this book because I wanted to create a single ultimate resource, containing all the tips, insights, and techniques that I have found helpful in my own journaling. Here my goal has been to bring practical information and emotional insight together in one place, so that you can find both suggestions for your journaling practice and ideas about how to use the fruits of your practice to gain greater self-awareness. Many books offer ideas to get you started with your journaling practice, but very few tell you how to make sense of what you discover.

On my own journey, I searched far and wide for a resource that explained the whole journaling process from start to finish, and that is what this book aims to do for you.

What Can Journaling Do for You?

Journaling puts you in touch with yourself. It helps you call on your inner strengths, lets you express the thoughts and feelings that you might not be able to express to anyone else

—perhaps because you feel they are too personal and too exposing. It's a record of your life. It is accessible any time of day, and you are totally in control of how much or how little time you spend on it. As a bonus, the act of journaling itself doesn't cost a thing.

Journaling has a range of emotional and physical benefits. According to the Yale Medical Group, regular journaling can help manage stress and anxiety, and aid people who are coping with depressive feelings. In an article published by an online psychology network called Psych Central ("The Health Benefits of Journaling," 2006), psychotherapist Maud Purcell suggested that the reason journaling can be so effective at helping us sort out our thoughts and feelings is because, when we write, our analytical, rational, and thinking left brain is busy, focused on the act of writing. This leaves our more intuitive, creative, and emotional right brain with space to make sense of our relationship with ourselves, other people, and to understand situations better. When the left brain is engaged, we take away the mental blocks this side of our brain erects to protect ourselves from the feelings or thoughts that challenge our self-beliefs or might be uncomfortable to explore.

Research at the University of Texas at Austin has shown that journaling can also have a positive influence on our physical well-being. Psychologist James W. Pennebaker, author of *Writing to Heal: A Guided Journal for Recovering from Trauma and Emotional Upheaval* (New Harbinger Publications, 2004) found that participants who engaged in a regular journaling practice experienced a strengthened immune system, as well as a reduction in physical symptoms caused by conditions like asthma and rheumatoid arthritis.

For me, I know that, without journaling, I would feel less than whole, because I would know less about myself.

Reading books, talking to other people, and similar activities are important and necessary to develop self-knowledge, but journaling is the most effective self-therapy tool I've encountered. Although I used to appreciate my journal because it was always there for me, I've come to realize I like it because it reminds me that *I* am always there for me.

You don't need to be a good writer and it doesn't matter if you don't consider yourself to be "creative." All the tools you need to start exist inside you already. The ideas and suggestions in this book are just suggestions, and you can tailor them as you wish.

How to Use This Book

This book is designed to be flexible. You can read it from start to finish or use it as a quick-reference guide. The first section explains journaling as a practice, including what tools to use, how frequently to do it, and how to get yourself in the right headspace to begin. The second and third sections contain a series of suggestions for written and using art for journaling. Finally, the fourth section explains how to use your journaling for greater insight into your past, present, and future. You'll find a list of resources at the back that are current at the time of writing. For a living list of resources (i.e. one that is regularly updated) relevant to this book, please visit www.becomingwhoyouare.net/guideto-journalingresources

You can use this book for the thirty-eight journaling ideas presented herein alone. Each numbered suggestion has its own chapter in Parts 3 and 4, so you can dip in and out as you need.

Each journaling suggestion's title summarizes the content and subject matter. When trying to choose one that feels right for you, try using the Contents page as a menu and start by exploring titles to which you feel drawn.

The ideas in this book aren't a substitute for professional help. If you feel like you're struggling with difficult feelings or thoughts, or want some support and guidance as you go through the exercises in the following pages, consider getting in touch with a licensed therapist or coach.

That's the skinny. I hope you enjoy reading and using this book as much as I've enjoyed writing it.

P.S. Before we move on, **would you like a free video class on starting (or restarting) your journaling practice?** If the answer is "Yes!" go to http://journaling.becomingwhoyouare. net/book and enter your email to access your free 10-step guide to starting a regular journaling practice. When you register, you'll also get more free workbooks, video classes and more tools for personal growth in the Becoming Who You Are Library (I will never, ever share your email and you are free to unsubscribe at any time).

PART 1
ALL ABOUT JOURNALING

WHAT IS JOURNALING?

Each time you make an entry into your journal, you open another door into yourself.
—*Lucia Capacchione, PhD*, The Well-Being Journal

In practice, journaling is whatever you want it to be. Underneath, it's the gateway to recording life, experiencing all manner of emotions, and uncovering parts of yourself you never thought existed.

But, you might think, *I already know everything I need to know about myself.*

Promise No. 1: I promise you, there's more.

Journaling can be fun. Writing about all the positive stuff leaves you feeling warm and fuzzy, and you can look back on the good times in years to come with a glowing nostalgia. But life isn't all nice, and journaling can also be nails-down-a-blackboard painful when it comes to the hard business.

When life gets uncomfortable, starts challenging our beliefs and assumptions, and leaves us feeling overwhelmed, it can feel more comfortable to retreat into "Dear Diary, had macaroni for lunch"-style journaling. That's not to say that the type of journaling you'll find here won't be deep and positive —it most certainly is. It's about getting past *what* happened, however, and getting to the *experience*, the *meanings*, and the *effects* underneath.

If you're looking for some proper pen-on-paper action—if you want to know more, be more and live a richer, more fulfilling life—keep reading. It's not all puppies and roses. When we journal, it can be uplifting, and we can also feel like we're being scrubbed across the washboard of unpleasant history and wrung through the ironing mangle of over-whelming emotion.

Exploring uncomfortable emotions, incidents, and facts can be challenging in all kinds of ways. So why do we do it?

Promise No. 2: If you commit to facing discomfort, you have the opportunity to reap big rewards.

Leaving the familiar and entering unfamiliar territory is a natural part of growth, but the unfamiliar can provoke discomfort, even fear. In order to deepen our self-awareness, we have to be willing to be uncomfortable.

Most of the suggestions in this book focus on written journaling (artists, there's a separate section for you too), but you don't have to stick to that format. Doodles, drawings, paintings, and other forms of art are just as helpful as the written word. The types of journaling you need might fluctuate from week to week. So go for whatever works for you when you sit down.

If it changes, stay curious; there are no rules about what you should or should not be writing or creating. *There is no right or wrong way to journal.* Many people have their own ideas about the right times to journal and writing methods to use, and I respect people's different preferences, so this book isn't prescriptive. Trust that your mind knows what it's doing, because it **does** know what it's doing.

The Benefits of Journaling

Most of our journaling focuses on how we relate to ourselves and others. We get to know the voices in our heads, the "parts" of our personality behind our raw emotions, and explore how these internal parts interact with each other. We learn more about our relationships with others and how we relate to them. We have the opportunity to turn around unhelpful patterns, improve our communication, and live more consciously.

There are parts of us that might never have had a chance to express themselves before now, parts that have been around for a long time but lie just below our conscious life. In childhood, we adapt our personalities, thoughts, and feelings to meet the needs of our caregivers. We have to; otherwise we risk emotional and physical rejection from the people we depend on. It's not something we consciously choose to do. Rather we inherently understand that if we don't conform we lose our caregivers' love, which, on a very primal level, could jeopardize our survival.

These parts have been waiting, since before you can remember, to speak their truth to someone who will hear them. What they have to say might not be pleasant, feel acceptable or comfortable, but they're part of you.

Without listening to these parts, they stay split off from our true selves. They come out in other ways: in acting out; in addiction (alcohol, drugs, or any other compulsive habit);

and in negative, untrue, and unquestioned beliefs about ourselves and others.

At the same time there might be hidden parts of us that feel what we'd describe as "positive" (or comfortable, pleasant) emotions. Just as we might grow up repressing feelings of hurt, anger, loneliness, and pain, sometimes our history might also lead us to suppress feelings and expressions of joy and happiness.

Journaling helps us give these parts a voice. It helps us tap in to their experiences, their feelings, and all the things they want to say. It helps us discover who we truly are. We can't negotiate with ghosts that we can't see, and, through journaling, these parts become visible. They no longer act out their beliefs and stories through unconscious actions that we can't explain and can't understand. Instead, we have a chance to develop an awareness and, eventually, acceptance of them.

How to Journal

So, that's what journaling is for, but how do we actually "do" journaling?

Journaling is a private act, so the way you go about it will be individual to you. You're the best judge of which journaling method is right for you, so it's not my place (nor anyone else's) to tell you how you should or shouldn't go about your practice. Here are three suggested guidelines to consider:

Be Honest - You might feel a range of comfortable and uncomfortable emotions during your journaling practice, and it's important to give all of these a voice. We can spend a lot of time in our everyday lives self-censoring, and your journal is the one place where you don't have to do that. Let loose, and see what comes out.

Forget about Grammar - This isn't an English exam, and no one else has to read what you've written. If you find yourself getting caught up in trying to shape your thoughts into perfectly formed sentences rather than just letting them flow, that might be something to explore in future journaling sessions.

Keep a Record - Add a date to every entry. This will make it much easier when you're retrospecting (see Part 4, Chapter 4) and is a great way of recording your life in detail. Imagine finding your journaling notes from today in 2030 and being able to look back to what was happening for you today. That would be pretty neat.

How do you feel about your journaling practice, having read this chapter?

Does the concept of having different internal parts resonate for you?

You can find more suggestions for starting and continuing a regular journaling practice on the resources page for this book: www.becomingwhoyouare.net/guidetojournalingresources

THE TOOLS AND TECHNIQUES OF THE TRADE

No one can give you better advice than yourself.
—Cicero

Tools

Journaling is traditionally a pen-and-paper activity, but any tool that allows you to express yourself freely is a good tool. You might start using one medium and switch to another in a few months. Perhaps you'll prefer using different tools for different types of journaling. The way you might want (or not want) to organize your thoughts and journaling will also influence what you use. My journaling implements have changed over the years. I alternate between being a note-book-and-pen person, to wanting to keep all my notes in one place in a digital format. I've met people who have separate notebooks for dreams, self-dialogues, and stream-of-consciousness journaling; people who put everything into a single notebook; as well as others who capture thoughts while out and about on 3x5 index cards.

Here is a list of different journaling tools to consider:

- Pen and paper
- Laptop or computer
- Lined notebook(s)
- Blank notebooks
- Dictaphone or other voice recorder
- Index cards
- Canvas
- Mood boards

Pen and Paper

Journaling isn't all about flashy fountain pens and Moleskine notebooks, but it could be. If you like the idea of pen and paper, you can work through notebooks (see below), or stick loose-leaf sheets of paper into ring binders. This takes up more space, but it also allows you to add drawings, writings, magazine or newspaper cuttings, and photos, as well as change the order of entries later if you wish.

Laptop

The digital age offers endless possibilities for journalers. Even the artists aren't left out, as software like Photoshop, Adobe Illustrator, and basic paint programs offer opportunities to get expressive. Plenty of software developers want to help as well. Macjournal, Day One and websites like 750 words.com can facilitate certain types of journaling. If you're traveling or want your journal to be accessible from anywhere around the world, Google Docs and Dropbox allow you to access the files online while keeping them under virtual lock and key with password protection.

If you choose online storage or journaling tools, you can hope your notes are private, but please don't assume they are shielded from prying eyes. The nature of the Internet means you never know who is watching, and hacks do happen, so engage with online services using a level of self-protection.

Notebooks, Lined or Blank

If you want to keep your journaling in one or more notebooks, you have several options to consider. Do you keep everything in one place and simply organize it chronologically? Or do you divide different thoughts into separate notebooks? Do you buy a notebook for a dollar or less? Or do you spend a little more time and money, carefully choosing a book with a beautiful cover and good quality paper? What size will it be? Do you want international sizes A4 (11.7x8.3 inches), A5 (5.8x8.3 inches), or a notebook the size of a reporter's pad? Do you want spirals or binding? Softback or hardback? Paper or leather? Horizontal or vertical binding?

For some people, a notebook is a notebook, and, as long as it's functional and portable, it'll do. Others see more significance in what the notebook represents. It might be your best friend for the next couple months or years. Perhaps you will tell it more about yourself and your life than you've ever told anybody. It could help you find out things about yourself that you never thought you'd know and reach depths you've never reached before. For these reasons, many people spend more time and money investing in a special journal that will be meaningful to them.

The writing implement is also important—will you pick up a ballpoint pen or invest in a fountain pen? Will you always use the same pen, will it depend on your mood, or will you simply use what's at hand?

Dictaphone

Voice recordings are helpful for people who are in a hurry, need to record things on the go, or want to record dreams or thoughts in the morning but are too sleepy to write coherent sentences. After falling asleep midsentence several times while writing down an action-packed dream, I was rescued by a Dictaphone. You might not even have to purchase a separate recorder, as many mobile phones now come with a voice memo function. Most recorders also allow you to transfer the voice files straight to your computer, where you can store them as you would a conventional written journal.

If you tend to think quickly or find it difficult to set aside time to sit down and write in privacy, a voice recorder might be just what you need. It's also interesting to listen back to the tone and emphasis of your voice—just like differences in your handwriting, this can tell you more about your thoughts and feelings at the time of recording.

Index Cards

Useful for capturing thoughts, notes, and ideas, index cards can be organized into categories or arranged in chronological order. Like voice memos, they allow you to take only what you need out and about with you, leaving your other notes in the safety of your home.

Techniques

Frequency

While I don't believe in "rules" for journaling, I do think some guidelines or suggestions will help optimize your writing, and frequency is one of these.

My frequency of journaling has fluctuated greatly from several times a day, to once every couple weeks. I try to do something every day but generally find that aiming for at least three sessions a week is a good guideline for me. It's not too demanding on my time, but it also helps me stay in touch with my thoughts and feelings. Any less frequently than that and I find that I start slipping back into old patterns of thinking, and my level of self-awareness dips. That's not to say that three times a week is the magic number. You will be able to establish your own minimum maintenance level and find out what works best for you. Overall, the more frequently you journal, and the more time you spend journaling, the more you'll benefit.

Journaling is a form of self-care. Just as we shower daily and carry out basic personal maintenance tasks like using a moisturizer, it's important to check in with ourselves mentally a few times a week. One way to think of journaling is like going to gym. You have to keep going a minimum number of times per week to maintain a certain level of fitness. The same applies to journaling for our emotional and mental health.

I don't always want to journal, and sometimes I feel a lot of resistance to sitting down and putting pen to paper, especially if I'm tired or have a lot on my plate. But, I know I'll feel better afterward though and much worse if I don't.

Time

Like frequency, the time of day you choose to journal will depend on your personal preferences. Your optimal time might be first thing in the morning or it could be last thing at night. There's no right or wrong choice here.

It's important to remember that the time of day you choose might have an impact on the type of journaling you do. I find that doing a stream-of-consciousness session in the morning is useful for clearing my head in preparation for the day to come. It's also a great time to record dreams while they're still fresh. The evening is perfect for reflection, for processing what has happened during the day, and for putting those events to rest before going to sleep. You can also set aside certain periods of time to journal on specific topics, or to help you work out situations, thoughts, or feelings that come up during the day. Of course your journaling might be affected by other factors, such as work and family commitments. As you journal, see which times of day feel more comfortable for you.

However busy you are, there will be a way for you to stay in touch with yourself, even if it's just making a two-minute "have done" list at the end of the day.

Privacy

One of the things I've found most challenging in my relationship with journaling is the idea of privacy or, more specifically, lack of privacy. For some people, journals are designed to be shared, while others are fiercely protective over their inner thoughts and feelings.

Some of us might come from homes where boundaries were not respected and where, as children, we had fewer rights to privacy than the adults around us. This leaves many wannabe journalers with a fear that their journal will be read by others. It's a difficult fear to live with, but we can remember that, as adults, we have full control over who reads our journal and who doesn't.

If you're concerned about privacy, you can take steps to preserve your thoughts and feelings, such as putting your notebook in a place where it won't be discoverable by others. You could also purchase a journal with its own lock and key. When journaling on a computer, programs like Day One let you add passwords, and you can even password-protect basic Microsoft Word files. Some dedicated journaling software (like Macjournal or Day One) also has an optional encryption feature, so, if your computer is ever lost or stolen, the data in your journaling files will appear scrambled, and no one will be able to see its contents.

I've heard a lot of debate around whether it's a good idea to show our personal journals to other people or not. Personally, I view my journal as private, and I think it's helpful to write with the assumption that you won't show anyone else. I might share parts of my journal in the future but, right now, it's just for me. If I think I'm writing for an audience—no matter how far in the future they're reading my journal—then I'll journal as though I'm writing for an audience. And that's not the point of journals. They are about your relationship with yourself, and for you only.

When we know there's a possibility we're not just writing for ourselves, we're at risk of self-censoring. Whether you choose to share your journal with someone in the future or not, I believe you will get to know yourself a lot better by writing for yourself only and not worrying about how your writing might look to others. The writing or art you produce isn't there to be judged by its content or quality. The main purpose is that you are true to yourself. If you want to produce something about yourself for other people to read, try writing a memoir, but keep your journals private.

Privacy, and the freedom that comes with it, is particularly important if you are writing about something secret, deeply personal, or something that leaves you feeling hurt, angry, or ashamed. Writing for ourselves, we can express our deepest fears and desires. Being able to do so without fear of judgment and rejection is an important part of the process. Remember that no one is there to judge you apart from yourself. Your journal is like a good therapist—it will not cast opinions or its own thoughts onto what you are writing. It is literally a blank page on which you can explore whatever you want and will reflect back to you what you have written. One way of thinking about your relationship with your journal is to imagine it as a boat from which you can dive, knowing that you can return to its safety whenever you choose.

You are the explorer, and your journal is the facilitator.

GETTING IN THE ZONE

Although to be driven back upon oneself is an uneasy affair at best... it seems to me now the one condition necessary to the beginnings of real self-respect.
—Joan Didion, "On Self-Respect"

Starting and maintaining a journaling practice can be more difficult than the actual journaling itself. Clearing our minds and finding a blank mental place from which we can begin journaling is challenging when everyday demands, tasks, and to-do lists are floating around our heads. Taking time to get into the "zone" enables us to explore topics with more depth and focus. It also allows us to approach our minds with respect, giving our thoughts and feelings the attention they deserve.

Finding the right kind of mind-set is a physical and a mental process. You might want to designate a journaling space, a particular place you reserve for your journaling sessions. Perhaps you choose to do it at your desk, in bed, or in the park. Although surroundings are important, the kind of environment you choose doesn't matter (although some privacy is helpful). The important thing is that it works for you. You might also find that your preferences change over time. Remember that you should ideally journal without any interruptions. These will distract your focus from your own thoughts and feelings, and prevent you from accessing the parts of yourself that usually stay hidden.

Introducing a ritual can also be helpful—whether it includes meditating, switching off your phone, or simply making a cup of tea before you start. If you enjoy journaling somewhere outside the home, in a café or a library, for example, your ritual can include your journey there.

Perhaps you enjoy having a certain type of music on in the background as you journal. I find music with lyrics distracting, as listening to the words takes my focus away from my thoughts, but I know others who also find it difficult to concentrate with silence. If you'd like background music during your journal practice, try finding some classical or ambient music. You can also download white-noise "nature" sounds, such as crashing waves or rain, which can be helpful for blocking out background chatter in public places.

Resistance

Getting into the journaling zone can be challenging the first few times you sit down to write. People find introspection difficult for a number of reasons: you might have a lot going on that takes your attention away from your journaling, or perhaps a part of you might resist facing some internal thoughts or emotions. An important aspect of journaling is finding peace and quiet to sit down and spend some time with ourselves. The key purpose of journaling is to be able to connect with ourselves—something which usually requires peace, quiet, and, ideally, solitude.

People who might be said to have "extroverted" personalities sometimes find it more difficult to introspect to begin with, as they process situations externally, not internally. An extrovert is more likely to talk as they think, while an introvert will think, then talk. Consequently thinking then journal writing is a process that can come more naturally to people who process the world in an introverted way than those who do so in an extroverted way.

Journaling can also be a challenge if you've never tried it before. You might find it difficult to get started, maintain focus, or think of something to write about. The first few times I journaled, I felt very self-conscious, and part of me was incredibly cynical about the whole exercise. It might take a while for you to feel comfortable with your practice, and this process can be uncomfortable and frustrating. But, if the initial challenges can be overcome, the benefits of journaling make any interim struggle totally rewarding. After all, it's worth some discomfort to have a better relationship with yourself and others rather than avoiding the discomfort in the short-term and never truly knowing yourself.

If you feel resistance to journaling, try asking yourself the following questions:

- How do I feel when I think of journaling?
- Do I feel uncomfortable about the idea of sitting in a room alone? If so, what is the thought behind this discomfort?
- What challenges do I think might come up if I start journaling?
- Is there something in my current life or history that's difficult to think about and might contribute to this resistance? If so, how could I approach this gently?
- How can I show compassion and empathy for myself during this process? Can I think of any potential

blocks to this compassion, and how am I going to deal with that?

Meditation

Meditation is a useful tool for clearing your mind of everyday matters in order to focus on what you'd like to write about. You can either do a guided meditation or simply sit, close your eyes, and breathe deeply for a few minutes, shifting your attention to your breath.

Some people find meditation easier than others. It can be hard to feel relaxed, particularly if there's a lot going on in your life or you feel some resistance to journaling. Don't worry if you get caught up in thinking. Just notice the thoughts, acknowledge them, and return your focus to your breathing.

Whether you feel meditation would be helpful for you or not, taking some deep breaths as you sit down to start journaling can help you feel more relaxed. If you don't have a particular topic in mind and, instead, are looking at what's going on in your life right now, the thoughts that come up as you focus on your breathing are a helpful starting point for your journaling.

PART 2

WRITTEN JOURNALING IDEAS

INTRODUCTION

Our worries can become less worrisome and our fears less fearful
when we write them down... Expressing private feelings on paper
can help to heal private hurts.
—*Gawain and Gayle J. Wells*

The number of techniques available to you as a journaler are
limited only by your creativity. As I've said, there are no rules
when it comes to journaling, and this is especially true for
the type of journaling you choose. This section contains
guidelines that outline thirty-eight different methods of
journal writing. They are, however, just a template you can
add to, take away from, and adjust to suit your goals and to
help you find the kind of journaling most beneficial to you.
The suggestions here aren't in any particular order, and you
certainly don't have to work through them one by one from
start to finish. Instead, return to the Contents page at the
beginning of this book and choose the one that appeals to
you the most right now.

Some of the suggestions in the following pages are adapta-
tions of other writers' and journalers' suggestions, and some

are my own. If you'd like to read more about journaling-related ideas and resources, please see the list of recommended reading under Further Resources at the end of this book or visit: www.becomingwhoyouare.net/guidetojour-nalingresources

1: DOMINANT AND NONDOMINANT HANDS

Most of us, apart from the ambidextrous, learn to write using either our left or right hands. The hand that we usually write with is called our dominant hand, and the hand we don't write with is called the nondominant hand. When we journal, we automatically use our dominant hand, as this is the hand we naturally turn to for writing tasks. Using our nondominant hand, however, is also a helpful tool, and you'll see several suggestions to try this in different contexts within the following pages.

Many journaling experts, such as Lucia Capacchione, author of *The Well-Being Journal*, believe that using the nondominant hand can help us access our inner child more easily than when writing with our dominant hands.

By adolescence and adulthood, we take the ability to write for granted. After all, we've been doing it for years. Writing using our nondominant hand takes us back to our time when that wasn't the case, a time in our childhood when we were still learning how to communicate with others. As well as reliving the sensation of what it felt like to learn how to write again, doing this can help us access the emotions from that time too.

You can try all the suggestions below writing with both your dominant and nondominant hands to see how you feel about the two different experiences.

2: THE ROAD NOT TAKEN

You might be familiar with the idea of the road not taken. It is the concept that, for every decision we make in life, there is an alternate path that we are leaving behind. Sometimes these decisions are easy—we'd much rather take one path than the other. Sometimes, however, they aren't; and making the decision between the two can feel tortuous.

This suggestion is similar to suggestion *26: Visualizations*, but it focuses on multiple possibilities, not just one.

To start, picture yourself ten years from now (you can use the visualization included in suggestion number 26 if it helps).

In as much detail as possible, write down everything you see in your visualization, ten years ahead. Helpful points to consider include:

- Where are you?
- What are you doing?
- Who are you with?

- What colors, smells, and senses are you experiencing?
- What is your work life like?
- What is your family life like?
- What kind of lifestyle do you have?
- What is the predominant feeling, ten years in the future?

Now, revisualize your future self. Imagine you are in an alternate universe, where you have taken different paths and traveled to a different place (literally or metaphorically speaking). Write down what you see, using the prompts above. This time, also consider:

- What are you doing in this alternate universe?
- What choices have you made to get there?
- How do you feel about those choices now?

You can carry on rewriting your visualization as many times as you want. You have endless possibilities in your life, so there are probably more outcomes than you immediately realize ...

3: BODY EVALUATION

This exercise can be challenging, particularly if you struggle with your appearance or have struggled in the past. If you know the subject of body image can trigger difficult feelings for you, consider doing the exercise with the help of a trusted friend or professional.

The body evaluation exercise is about facing which parts of our bodies we like and why, and which parts of our bodies we don't like and why.

Start by standing in front of a mirror and examine each part of your body in turn, beginning with your head and ending with your feet. With each part, ask yourself:

- How do I feel about this part I'm looking at and why?
- What emotions are connected with this part?
- Have any people or experiences influenced the way I feel about this part?

After your initial body evaluation, you can dialogue with any parts of your body you don't feel so comfortable about (see *9: Dialogues*), using your dominant and nondominant hand.

4: BODY EXPERIENCES

A lot of personal development work we do around our bodies is related to self-image and how we feel about our appearance. While that is valuable, sometimes it leaves *physical* experiences overlooked. These are just as important, and this suggestion looks at ways to excavate and explore them.

Just like emotional trauma can affect our bodies, bodily trauma can deeply affect our emotions. When we experience physical trauma, we're often so caught up in our physical healing that we neglect its emotional impact. This journaling suggestion can help access and open up those emotions.

It involves creating a body reflections timeline or chart that helps you map out major illnesses or physical events that have occurred in your life so far.

A basic timeline should consist of the date, a description of the illness, accident, or injury (including which part/parts of your body it affected), and the physical and emotional feelings that went with it. You might find it helpful to separate this information in a table format, or you can write each event as a separate journal entry.

To fully access emotions, experiment with completing this exercise in the present tense, instead of the past. You can also try writing the chart out with your nondominant hand.

Example Timeline:

January 2000 - Broken arm

I was skating at my local ice rink as part of a friend's birthday celebration and slipped on the ice. My arm felt strange, painful, yet disembodied. I knew something was wrong. Wearing a cast and waiting for the break to heal was frustrating, and I felt weaker. This was the first time I had broken anything, and it felt like a shock to realize that I could. Somehow I felt more mortal after the experience.

5: BODY REEVALUATION

Body reevaluation is a simple yet thought-provoking exercise. It involves taking a negative belief or feeling about our body, reframing it as an alternative belief, and thinking about what we have to do to bridge the gap between the two.

You can do this as a written exercise or using a more art-based format.

Example Reevaluation:

Negative belief/feeling: I don't like my stomach.

Alternative belief/feeling: My stomach looks exactly the way it's supposed to.

Actions: Showing self-care about what foods I choose to put in my stomach.

Creating positive affirmations.

Taking time to look at my stomach each day and focusing on the alternative belief/feeling.

6: CHARACTER SKETCHES

Character sketches help you focus on what you think and feel about other individuals. They can also help you explore what you think these people feel about you. This type of journaling is useful for examining your relationships with the people you have in your life, and it can also help you reflect on how others might see you.

You don't have to ask friends, family, and coworkers for feedback to do this exercise, as it's actually more helpful to do it alone. It's about being able to empathize with other people's perceptions and reflect on the verbal and nonverbal feedback they have given you.

If I were writing a character sketch about my friend Bob, I would start by writing down the different thoughts and feelings I have about him. Then I would write a piece from his perspective, as if he were doing the same exercise but writing about me. Thinking about how others perceive us is a key part of personal growth. It can be a little uncomfortable, but it can also be validating and confidence-boosting too.

You can do character sketches for anyone: friends, family, coworkers, teachers, students, neighbors, clients, therapists. The possibilities are only limited by the number of relationships. The important thing is to choose someone specific. Writing about "my friends" or "my family" isn't going to be helpful, as the groups we call our friends and family consist of different individuals, each of whom we experience and relate to in a different way.

Ideas for Character Sketches

- Mother
- Father
- Brother
- Sister
- Individuals from extended family: aunts, uncles, cousins, grandparents, etc.
- Partner
- Ex-partner
- Boss
- Individual coworkers
- Individual friends
- Individual neighbors

7: CHEERLEADING

This suggestion focuses on taking negative thoughts or beliefs we have about ourselves and turning them around. It's about developing your inner cheerleader, the part of you that is 100 percent on your side and thinks you are the bee's knees.

This part is particularly important if we have a strong inner critic. If your inner critic is very vocal, this exercise might feel alien and unnatural at first; however, the more frequently you practice, the stronger your inner cheerleader will grow.

To start, take a negative thought or belief you have about yourself:

I'm not very good at tennis. I have no natural talent, and everyone I play with is better than me.

Turn it around from a negative to a positive:

I try really hard at tennis, and I'm getting better all the time. The more I play, the more skilled I become and the more confident I feel.

This exercise is simple, and it's also very powerful. When we have negative beliefs or thoughts about ourselves, these can become self-fulfilling. Therefore, if I believe I am not very good at tennis, the chances are that I'll play as though I'm not very good, regardless of my actual skills and capabilities.

For this journal entry, think of something you are critical about and start writing about that thing, as though it is exactly what it needs to be, and it is totally acceptable to you.

What do you notice?

8: DEALING WITH UPSET AND WORRY

Whenever we are distractingly upset or worried about something, this could be because our inner child has been triggered and is now dominating our other main parts, the parent and adult (see *The Inner Child and Dissociation* for more information on these concepts).

When certain parts of ourselves get triggered and enter this tunnel-vision-like state, it can be difficult to right the balance between our internal parts again. Creating a dialogue between our inner child and our nurturing inner adult can restore equilibrium between the two parts and helps foster our self-soothing capabilities.

Begin by closing your eyes and focusing on your breathing. Either internal part of you can start the dialogue. Simply go with what feels right to you. The upset and anxious part might have a lot to say to begin with, or you might find that the nurturing part comes forward to initiate the conversation.

When writing this dialogue, you can encourage each part to come forward by using your dominant writing hand for the adult voice and your nondominant writing hand for the child's. You can also journal to resolve upset and worry using a computer (although you won't be able to differentiate between dominant and nondominant hand using this method).

This technique is useful for when you're feeling stressed or anxious, as it can help you explore and process what's happening for you, helping you reach clarity and, eventually, equilibrium.

9: DIALOGUES

If you've done some journaling before, you might have already identified some of the different voices that appear in your thoughts. With dialogues, you give these voices a chance to speak.

Dialogues can take the form of a question-and-answer conversation between two different parts, or a distinct part of your personality and your "self." Conducting a dialogue between different internal parts gives them a chance to be heard—perhaps a chance to listen too. One type of dialogue could be a conversation between two conflicting parts, for instance, a critical part and also a hurt, fearful child part afraid of the criticism.

You can also explore certain parts of your personality through monologue, allowing a part to express fully its thoughts and feelings about a certain subject without any other parts stepping in to argue or dismiss.

Dialogues aren't limited to parts of your internal world. You can try dialoguing with parts (or all) of your body, objects, or abstract concepts, for example "career" and "the future."

Holding dialogues with your body helps you uncover your genuine thoughts and feelings about your appearance and self-care. Doing so with concepts like "career" and "the future" enables you to learn more about what the different parts of you think about these big topics.

We know what we *should* think and feel about these things; so, when we explore them, our ego can get in the way. Having one or more dialogues with your body helps get past the ego and to the real feelings underneath. This same principle applies to other topics, such as life choices, food, exercise, and so on.

The purpose of dialogues is to give every voice in your head a chance to be heard without judgment or repression. Some of the thoughts and topics that come up might be uncomfortable to deal with at first, but remember that this is only a part of you that thinks this—the thoughts and feelings emerging do not represent you as a whole. Just because one part of you has a thought that another part of you labels as "bad," it doesn't mean you are a "bad" person. A key reason for using dialogues in journaling is that they help us identify and negotiate conflicts between different parts, understanding where they come from, why they feel the way they do, and working with them all together.

If you're having trouble identifying your internal voices, take your time. There's no set method for recognizing and differentiating between the various voices in the choir, but trying to visualize the character behind an individual voice can be helpful for building an image. You can try asking the following questions:

- What is the voice's name?
- What gender is it?
- How old is it?

- What does it look like?
- What are three adjectives that describe its character?
- Does it remind you of anyone you know?

You can find several starting points for dialogues under A List of Prompts at the end of this section.

Sample Dialogue

The concept of dialogues can feel quite alien, especially if you are not used to thinking of your personality in terms of "parts." To give you an idea of what a dialogue might look like, here is a conversation with my inner Victorian governess. The name of this part might sound strange, even slightly comical, but I call her this because she is strict and is a part of my personality that wants to deny me things she calls "luxuries." Sometimes these are things I actually need; other times they are things I would like to have or do for self-care purposes. When this part is in the driver's seat, I feel guilty about treating myself with care, which conflicts with other parts of me that need to feel nurtured. Here is an edited version of one of our dialogues:

Me: Hello.

VG: Hello, Hannah.

Me: I would like to talk to you about the things you say when I want to do something nice for myself.

VG: Go ahead.

Me: When I want to take time off and do something nice, like go for a walk or spend money on something, I feel guilty when you tell me that it's wrong. I see other people rewarding themselves and doing things, like buying new clothes and taking joy in that, and I can't.

VG: Do you think that's my problem?

Me: I don't know. I think so, but I'm trying not to reach any conclusions. Like I said, I see other people doing it. I know it's normal to want to do this, and I want to be able to do it myself. I want to be able to go and sit in a park and read on a Saturday afternoon without feeling like I'm doing something wrong or being lazy.

VG (interrupting): Well, it is lazy.

Me: Can I just finish?

(The conversation continues; I explain my experience and how I feel, then start asking questions. She reveals that she is trying to protect me from other people's criticisms.)

Me: But you know that I feel unhappy when you call me names, like *lazy*. Do you realize that the way you're trying to stop other people from behaving badly to me is by behaving badly to me yourself?

VG: Well, that's different.

Me: How?

VG: Because I'm part of you, I care about you.

Me: Whoa. OK. So you say you care about me, but you call me names, and you tell me that I don't deserve nice things.

VG: It's not quite like that …

Me: Yes, it is. That's my experience of it. I need a break sometimes. I need to have fun, and I need to enjoy life. I would love to make the most of the world, and I would like to do that with you on my side. Are you willing to talk about this some more in the future?

VG: Sure. I think what you say makes sense. I don't know how I feel about it. I want to say you're wrong, but I'm not sure. I'll talk to you again.

Me: I would like that. Thank you.

As you can see, dialogues aren't a one-time event, and you might need to have several before both voices feel understood. Whenever you finish a dialogue with an internal part or area of your body, it's important to thank them for their time, so they feel heard.

10: DREAMS

Dreams are a treasure trove of useful information about our thoughts, feelings, experiences, and desires. They are our brain's way of processing events that have happened and things we have learned. They can be pleasant, confusing, funny, disturbing, and just plain bizarre. Dreams provide a helpful window into what's happening in our unconscious, especially when viewed alongside the journaling we do during our waking hours.

Recording and decoding my dreams is one of my favorite journaling exercises. I find it fascinating to see what's going on in my unconscious and how it relates to events in my history and current life.

There are many conflicting theories about how dreams work and what they mean. I've personally found that they can be incredibly helpful for exploring how my mind is processing information and can help reveal a lot about thoughts or feelings buried under the surface.

Your dreams might be vivid, hazy, metaphorical, and/or sense-based. Sometimes the images might be more memorable. At other times it might be visceral emotions that stay with you the most. You might experience a powerful sense of smell or touch, or perhaps there is a sound track, background noise, or certain dialogue that stays with you from the dream. While I don't wholly believe in dream dictionaries or universal symbols, I do think that different images have significance in different ways for each of us.

Some people find it difficult to remember their dreams, either because they fall back to sleep and then can't remember the dream upon waking, or because they don't think they dream at all. I struggled with the former situation, until I started using a voice recorder. I found that speaking uses far less energy and time than writing, so I could mumble my few thoughts into the microphone before giving in to the temptation to sleep.

If you experience difficulty recalling your nap-time musings, start by writing down or recording your waking thoughts and feelings. Show your mind you are listening, and it will usually respond. Many people who previously were certain they didn't dream found that this provoked a stream of vivid nighttime adventures. Even the simple act of asking for a dream before going to sleep can be enough to let your mind know that you are ready to hear and to take note of what it has to say.

When I look at dreams, I start by thinking about the major events or issues occurring in my life at present. These might include job changes, relationships, or whether anything happening in my life evokes any strong feelings. I also think about what happened the day before the dream, including the people I met, places I visited, and what was on my mind.

Many of our dreams contain characters. We might recognize some of them as people we know in real life, and others might be complete strangers. Whoever they are, it's important to remember that they appeared in your dream; therefore, you created them. Think about who each character might represent—they could be people from your past or present, or even symbolize part of your own personality.

Dream interpretation can be difficult at first, but, once you become familiar with the way your unconscious processes information, it's easier to unravel even the most confusing dreams. Some people become very good at interpreting their own dreams, but it can also be useful to ask for feedback from others. Dreams are incredibly personal, so talk to people you can trust and with whom you feel comfortable sharing intimate information.

As well as a straight interpretation, you can use your dreams as a starting point for an array of other journaling exercises. These include starting a dialogue with the characters in the dream. Try using your dominant hand for your portion of the narrative and your nondominant hand for the narrative of the character.

11: FINDING MEANING

In *A Creative Guide to Exploring your Life* (Jessica Kingsley Publishers, 2008), authors Graham Gordon Ramsey and Holly Barlow Sweet define *meaning* as "that which gives us a sense of purpose." Here are a few questions and prompts you can use to start exploring meaning in your life:

1. What does meaning look like in your life?

2. What activities or elements in your daily life give you sense of purpose?

3. What is your biggest current obstacle to feeling purposeful? What can get in the way of experiencing meaning?

4. What is one thing you could start doing, or do differently, that would add a greater sense of purpose to your life?

12: FINISH THE STORY

Dealing with uncertainty is one of the realities of life. Some people thrive on uncertainty, enjoying the fact that they don't know what lies ahead. Others (like me) shrink away from it, attempting to find an answer to an unresolved issue or situation as quickly as possible, even if it means making a decision before we have all the relevant information.

Finish the Story is about visualizing and creating an ending or resolution that you want. To start, describe an upcoming or current scenario that feels unresolved or where you don't know what's going to happen.

Then write down all the different outcomes that you think might occur, no matter how ridiculous or unlikely they seem. Finally choose one or two outcomes that would be ideal.

How do you think you can facilitate these chosen outcomes?

Example:

Unresolved situation:

Two of my biggest clients have recently said they won't be requesting any more work this season. This leaves a hole in my monthly budget, and, as yet, I don't know how to fill it.

Options:

Do nothing and hope for the best.

Apply for as many projects as possible per day and prioritize this over other activities.

Approach previous clients and let them know I am available.

Use the extra time to improve my website.

Give up.

Apply for a part-time job to fill the gap.

Pack in freelancing altogether and go for a full-time, seemingly more stable gig.

Extend my overdraft.

Cut down all unnecessary expenses.

Ideal choices:

Apply for as many projects as possible.

Approach previous clients.

Cut down expenses.

13: FREE ASSOCIATION

Free association is similar to stream-of-consciousness journaling; however, it involves single words rather than complete trains of thought.

Start with a word or topic, then write down all the words you associate with it. Don't overthink or analyze what comes up while you're journaling—there are no right or wrong answers, and everything is acceptable.

When you can't think of any more words, look back at what you've written. Ask yourself:

Do you notice any patterns in the words you wrote down?

Notice any thoughts and feelings that came up while writing?

Did some words sit more comfortably with you than others?

A variation on this exercise is to try chain-reaction free association. This involves writing down the first word you associate with the previous one you have written. It's like a shorthand version of stream-of-consciousness journaling, and it's often interesting to see where your mind takes you!

Some examples of starting prompts for free association include:

- Food
- Money
- Appearance
- Career
- Family
- Relationships
- Sex
- Love
- Loneliness
- Separation
- Solitude
- Companionship
- Life
- Death
- Beginning
- Ending

Example:

Food

meal

hard

portion

size

weight

meat

allergy

difficult

choices

fridge

freezer

life

needs

greens

vitamins

nutrition

taste

hunger

carbohydrates

energy

relationship

Patterns: a mix of positive and negative.

Emotions: uncomfortable, guilty, sensitive, intrigued.

14: EXPLORING GENDER

Gender is something that affects all of us in ways we're not even aware of perhaps. The gender we are born into greatly influences our experiences and perceptions of the world, yet we rarely stop to question what it means to us to be one of our gender.

As a starting point for exploring gender, it's helpful to make three lists of all the cultural stereotypes you're aware of that are associated with men, women, and transgender. You can also write down the feelings that each stereotype evokes for you and how you feel about typical cultural perceptions of your gender.

Other questions you might want to use as a starting point for exploring gender and your feelings around this topic include:

- How do you think your life would be different if you were born into another gender?
- Do you identify with any stereotypes typically attributed to a different gender? If so, what is it about these stereotypes you identify with, and how do you feel about that?

- Do you recognize any "feminine" or "masculine" parts of your personality? If so, what words and feelings do you associate with them?
- Are there any characteristics, behaviors, or mannerisms you have because that's how people of your gender are expected to behave? Or is there something you want to do but avoid, because it wouldn't match society's perception of your gender?
- Imagine a world where your society's gender roles didn't exist and where the only difference between men and women was biological. Would your life be different? If so, how?

15: GRATITUDE JOURNAL

A gratitude journal is a great way of injecting some feel-good vibes into your day. You can experiment with keeping many different kinds of gratitude journals, including lists of ten things you're grateful for, unsent letters to people you're grateful to, and so on. The idea of keeping a gratitude journal is popular, and you can find different examples of this kind of journal online. However you choose to create your gratitude journal, it can help you see life from a different perspective. Gratitude journals are especially helpful during tough times, if you are dealing with difficult situations or events, or simply want to focus on the positive aspects of life a little more.

Gratitude List Example:

List of ten things I'm grateful for right now:

My health

My Mac

My partner

Holidays

Good music

Fruit salad

Coffee

My current novel

Being able to work and travel

A warm sweater on an autumn day

16: NURTURE LIST

Nurturing and self-care involves people, places, and things that nurture our physical, emotional, mental, and spiritual needs.

This is often something that comes secondary to other activities and priorities in our lives. Generally, women are taught that self-care comes after caring for other people, while men are taught that they don't need self-care for they are to be strong at all times.

Self-care and nurturing, however, are crucial to our happiness. Women cannot truly care for others until they can show themselves care; and, when men deny their need for self-care, they are denying something very basic and necessary.

If we aren't used to making time for self-care, we need to make a conscious effort to do so. You can find more information about creating a self-care practice that works (plus dozens of practical suggestions) in my book *From Coping to Thriving: How to Turn Self-Care Into a Way of Life.*

For now, journaling can be a helpful way to list self-care activities we can use to nourish ourselves and even scheduling time for these activities into our calendars.

In my experience, there are two types of activities that fall under the self-care category: those that we know are good for us but don't enjoy (such as going to the dentist), and those that we know are good for us and feel like bliss (such as lying in bed and reading a book all morning).

To differentiate between these activities, I will call the first group *self-care activities*, and the second *self-nurturing activities*. So that you can capture the activities good for you which you enjoy, as well as those less pleasurable in the short-term, divide these into two lists. For every item on list one, self-care activities, add an item to the self-nurturing list two to balance out the *good and not-so-pleasurable* with the *good and pleasurable*.

Here are some items that might fall under the self-care list:

- Going to the dentist
- Going running
- Getting vaccinations
- Studying a voluntary subject to further personal development (e.g., learning a language as an adult)
- Eyebrow plucking/leg shaving/other personal maintenance
- Getting a medical exam
- And here are some that might fall under the self-nurturing list:
- Sleeping in
- Getting a haircut
- Buying a new item of clothing to replace a worn-out or ill-fitting one
- Doing gentle yoga stretches

- Having a warm bath
- Doing something creative or artistic, such as painting, drawing, or making jewelery
- Making time to read a good book

If you get stuck for ideas, try visualizing your ideal day or half day off from work, chores, or other commitments. What would you do with your time, and how would you feel? You can also experiment with writing your self-care and self-nurture lists with your nondominant hand. Your list should be uncensored and can contain anything, from the completely banal to the totally crazy. Remember that you're not obligated to do anything on it. The process is a brain-storm session rather than a list of things you're committing to doing.

Once you have your lists, review list one (the self-care list) regularly to see if anything on there needs attention (is it time for a checkup?) Every time you act on an item from list one, remember to balance it out with something from list two. Choose as many items per week from list two as you feel you need.

17: PHOTOS

Photos are a record. They capture a single moment in time and provide a reminder of that moment long after it has passed.

We take photos for all kinds of reasons. Often we take them in order to not forget. We might be at a special event or occasion, and we want to remember it in the future. Sometimes photos are just taken, not for any particular or special reason, but they are a snapshot of everyday life.

Whatever the case, photos are a wonderful tool for journaling. To use photos, select one taken six months ago or more.

Study the photo, and use the following questions for reflection:

- How do you feel when you look at it now?
- Can you remember what was happening when it was taken and how you felt at the time?
- Does the picture evoke any other memories?
- Has time changed the way you view and experience this picture? If so, how?

18: PRACTICAL JOURNALS

Practical journals tell us in measured, objective terms what our life today is like. Examples of practical journals include a mood journal and a food journal.

A mood journal involves tracking your feelings through the day. You might choose to make a note of how many times per day you feel a certain emotion, such as anxiety or anger. Alternatively you might decide to record what emotions you feel at certain times of the day, for example, 9:00 a.m., 12:00 p.m., 3:00 p.m., 6:00 p.m., and 9:00 p.m. This is helpful for getting a clearer picture about your mood cycles and what kind of situations or events trigger certain moods. When making an entry in your mood journal, you can also include the thoughts you are having at the time, as it's useful to later reflect on how your thoughts might be influencing your moods.

A food journal is useful if you want to pay more attention to the amount you're eating or the balance in your diet. Writing down what you eat and drink, especially in conjunction with your mood, can help reveal patterns that previously might have been unconscious.

Other examples of practical journals can include money journals (when you spend money, how much you spend, what you spend it on, and how you feel when you spend it), and word journals (noticing when you use certain words or verbal tics and why).

Practical journals can also be combined, especially if you feel one factor might influence the other. For example, if you tend to spend money when you feel upset or anxious, try keeping a combined money and mood journal.

Some people find it effective keeping practical journals for a few days to a week; however, if you want to get a thorough overview of the area of your life that you're tracking, consider keeping the journal for one to three months and reviewing it on a regular basis to look at any developing patterns.

19: SPRINGBOARDS

Like prompts, springboards are useful if you want to journal, but the words just aren't flowing. Springboards are prompts from your everyday life and provide a starting point for a private journaling discussion.

As we go through the day, we are constantly seeing images, hearing sounds, and meeting people who trigger certain feelings, ideas, memories, or thoughts. It might not be appropriate or useful to explore them at that moment, but, if you jot them down, you can return to them later when you have more time and privacy. Springboards can be questions or statements, although I have found the latter more useful for getting in touch with my feelings and thoughts.

Examples of Springboards:

Today I am …

I am happiest when …

I feel sad when …

Today I noticed I felt …

What I like about myself is …

What I like about [insert name of friend/partner here] is …

20: ROLES

We all play a multitude of roles in our lives, each of which require different skills plus need different things from us. Often we slip into these roles without thinking too much about them and the effects they might have on us. Sometimes, however, a single role can overwhelm us, and we can start self-identifying with that role as a core part of who we are.

The fact is, we are all many people at once. We are not just one thing to one person, but we have many roles for different people in our lives.

Try creating a monologue from the perspective of each of the roles you play. This might be as a mother, father, son, daughter, employee, boss, partner, spouse, friend, sibling, etc. Ask yourself:

- What do you notice about each of the roles you play?
- How closely is each role aligned with your "ideal" self, the person you would like to be?
- Are there any differences between the tone and content in each monologue?

- How do you feel when reading back each monologue?

21: THE EULOGY

The idea of writing your own eulogy isn't meant to be grim; it's a way to gain clarity on what you want to do with your life. Thinking about how we want others to remember us after we die is one of the most powerful ways we can work out what is really important to us.

When writing your eulogy, do so in the third person. Include everything you can think of that you'd like people to remember about you. Start with your personality, then move on to what you did and experienced in your life.

How does your eulogized life compare to the life you're living now?

A variation on this exercise, which has a similar purpose, is to write a journal entry as though you have one week, month, or year to live. How would you feel if you knew how long you had? What would you do with your limited time?

Sometimes the results from this exercise are surprising, especially when we compare them to the way we spend our time now.

22: STREAM OF CONSCIOUSNESS

Stream-of-consciousness journaling is useful for clearing your head of mental clutter and working through unresolved internal conflicts. With this kind of journaling, you simply write whatever comes into your head—no matter what it might be. The thoughts don't have to be logically connected, easy to read, or grammatically correct; it doesn't even have to make sense.

With stream-of-consciousness journaling, try not to force certain thoughts. Just write about whatever comes to mind. Although it might be difficult not to judge what you are writing as you go, put aside those thoughts and save them for later. In the meantime, remember that everything is acceptable. Nothing is too boring, bad, violent, blue, evil, trivial, etc. It's all part of you, so it's OK to express.

Later on in the day, week, month, or year, return to what you have written. As you're rereading, look for any patterns or notable imagery, and revisit what was on your mind and how you were feeling when you were writing this.

It might be useful to aim for a minimum word count; it might not. Experiment and see what works best for you. Websites such as 750 words.com offer a helpful template. If you don't write much, producing 750 words might seem impossible at first, so start with less words and build up, even if it means pushing yourself beyond your comfort zone.

23: PROMPTS

Prompts are useful for leading your mind down the rabbit hole, especially when you're not sure what to journal about or maybe want to explore new ideas you haven't written about before. You can make your own list of prompts, use the prompts included in A List of Prompts (suggestion 30), later in this part of the book, find other prompts online that focus on a certain topic, or explore sentence-completion exercises.

Sentence-completion prompts are slightly different from traditional journaling prompts, but the thoughts and feelings that come up as you complete the exercise can provide useful material for journaling. I've found sentence completion so effective for my own personal development that I created a separate book and course around it (for more information, take a look at 4 Weeks of Self-Knowledge, which is available through Becoming Who You Are).

Visual stimuli also work as prompts. You can use photos, images, or videos as a starting point for your journaling. If you have photos from the past (anytime from your childhood up to the last eighteen months), lay them out in chronological order, then create a journal entry about each one or your impressions of a set. Notice details, like locations, facial expressions, and body language. If you're in the photo with other people, think about what your relationship was like with them at the time. Is this relationship still the same, or has it changed since the photo was taken? What is your emotional reaction to seeing the photo now?

Prompts might consist of a sentence or provide a more detailed overview of what to write about. Either way they are most beneficial when you include as much detail in your answer as possible. With shorter prompts, your initial answer might consist of a sentence or even just a word. You can leave it there but explore the topic as deeply as possible and see where your mind takes you.

Prompt Suggestions:

- Something I remember from last summer.
- An unresolved issue.
- An unfulfilled dream.
- How I'll make my millions.
- A memorable read.

If you'd like a year's worth of daily prompts to inspire your journaling practice, I invite you to take a look at *The Year of You: 365 Journal Writing Prompts for Creative Self-Discovery.*

24: STEPPING STONES

Stepping stones is a method of journaling that was developed by Dr. Ira Progoff (who created a course called the Intensive Journal Program).

The basic premise is that you start at the beginning of your life with "I was born" and list the key events that happened after that. These might include things like the birth of a sibling, marriage, the death of a parent, and so on.

Kathleen Adams, author of *Journal to the Self* (Grand Central Publishing, 1990), suggests dividing the stepping stones into four categories: heart, mind, spirit, and body. Then write a list for each. The heart list might contain a list of feelings that occurred at different stages of your life, while the mind list will be more factual. The spirit list focuses on the intuitive aspects of life: Were you ever religious? How has your relationship with your spiritual side changed? Lastly the body list might involve things like reaching puberty, having children, gaining or losing weight, and thoughts or actions associated with your body.

Each stepping stone then acts as a springboard, with which you can explore each item more deeply. Some of your stepping stones might include years' worth of content; others might focus on a single event or moment in time. Adams suggests starting with "It was a time when ..." to get you going.

25: TURNING POINTS

Turning points are defining moments in your life that changed your perspective of someone important, the way you view yourself, or the world. These could be cultural events, such as 9/11 or the Arab Spring, or events very personal to you. It's useful to look at both personal and cultural landmarks. Our self-history is important, but it's only part of the picture. When exploring our experiences, beliefs, and feelings, it's also helpful to look at our personal history within a wider historical, social, and cultural context.

With each turning point, consider describing:

- What happened?
- How did it affect you at the time?
- How does it affect you now?
- What did you learn about yourself?
- What did you learn about others?
- What would you say to yourself, if you could go back in time?

You can also include key figures in your life as turning points. For each person, try thinking about:

- How you knew/know them.
- How they influenced you.
- Key messages they passed on to you.
- What you thought about them (and still think, if you know them today).
- How you felt about them (and still feel, if you know them today).

26: VISUALIZATIONS

Visualizations are useful for looking into the future. When you journal around a visualization, it might focus on a very specific situation, such as what you want from your career, personal life, or family. Alternatively the focus might be more general. For instance, where do I think I'll be in a year's time?

We all have future aspirations and plans, but often we get so caught up in everyday life that it can be difficult to really focus on where we want to be heading. We usually have ideas about what we want to do and where we want to end up, but visualizations help turn vague images into detailed pictures. Recording your visualizations not only brings your goals to the front of your mind, enabling you to make better decisions now to help you achieve them, but it can be interesting to chart the way your visualizations change over time.

If you're not sure how to journal using visualizations, you might find it helpful to start with the template below.

Visualization Template

This is a short introductory visualization. It's designed to help you look one year ahead, but you can adapt the exercise to look five and ten years ahead too.

Sit comfortably in your chair with your feet on the ground. Close your eyes and take several long, deep breaths, in and out ...

As you breathe, relax your body. Start with your face, move to your shoulders, on to your stomach and hips, and finally your legs and feet.

Try not to focus on any thoughts in particular. As you breathe, thoughts will come into your head, but let them come and go without trying to control anything.

Keep breathing deeply.

You know where you are right now.

Think forward to one year from now. Just sit with how you feel in the future. Now imagine opening your eyes at that point in time, one year in the future.

Where are you? Are you inside or outside? What do your surroundings look like? Take in and notice colors, shapes, and objects. Can you smell anything? What can you hear around you? You don't have to provide answers for all these questions. Simply notice sights, sounds, and sensations as they come.

Now think about your life in this future. What job do you have? Is it the same or different from what you are doing now? Think about your social life. What friends do you have around you? Are you in a relationship? If so, who is it with?

Now think about how you spend your time. Think of the things you do, when you're not at work, on the weekends or in the evenings.

What does your home look like? Are you still living in the same place, or have you moved? What does the place look like? Do you live with anyone else? Think about the environment—the colors, the smells, and the way the place feels. What do you notice about it?

Next look at yourself and what you have achieved up to this point in the future. What is different now compared to twelve months ago? Have any notable events happened?

Keep focusing on what you can sense, the images that pop into your head, and take note of any sensations in your body. How do you feel thinking of these images?

Keep breathing deeply, focusing on how you feel. When you are ready, open your eyes in three ... two ... one ...

Now spend as long as you need writing a description of what you saw. Include as much detail as possible, thinking about all five of the senses: sight, sound, smell, taste, and touch.

It might be helpful to repeat this exercise, or an adapted version, on a semiregular basis—for instance, every month or every few months—to see how your visualizations of the future evolve. The more detailed your picture is, the easier it will be for you to translate it into actionable goals that will help you achieve the future you want.

For a more powerful visualization, you can also try writing down what you saw in the present tense, as though it were already happening or you were experiencing it at this very moment.

27: UNSENT LETTERS

Unsent letters can contain all the things we could say to someone but wouldn't feel comfortable doing. Either we don't feel confident enough, are afraid of the repercussions, or simply haven't had the chance. With unsent letters, we have an opportunity to express our true feelings to someone about our relationship with them, or situations and events that have occurred, without actually having to reveal our feelings face-to-face.

You can write unsent letters to your parents, siblings, friends, ex-partners, current partners, bosses, colleagues, as well as anyone else who has impacted, or continues to impact, your life in a positive or negative way.

You can also write unsent letters discussing your feelings to body parts, illnesses, pets, inanimate objects, situations, and events. This might not feel so natural at first, but it can help you to express your feelings about illnesses, injuries, important events, and other things that have significance in your life.

It might feel like there's not much point in writing a letter if you're not going to send it. With unsent letters, however, it's not about the other person ever hearing or receiving what we want to say. Instead, the letter is a method through which we can explore our true experiences and our feelings about a certain person, event, situation, or thing. It's an exercise for our individual benefit only and no one else's. Writing an unsent letter helps us clarify our feelings, without having to worry about what would happen if the person or people involved saw the letter. It's about expressing our feelings, not about censoring what we write to save someone else from hurt feelings.

To begin an unsent letter, start by addressing the person, as you would in a normal letter:

Dear Harry,

Then write everything you wish you could say to that person, without self-censorship or fear that they might read it—they won't. When you're finished, leave the letter for a few days, then read it again. What do you notice?

28: LISTS

Lists are one type of journaling I really enjoy, and a perfect technique to start with if you feel self-conscious about writing prose. Lists are a fun practice, and they're also great for building a deeper awareness of yourself: your likes, dislikes, thoughts, and opinions.

Kathleen Adams, author of *Journal to the Self* (Grand Central Publishing, 1990), talks about making lists of one hundred. As the name suggests, you focus on your chosen topic and write down whatever comes into your head until you have a list of one hundred items. She suggests making each list in one sitting, but I've also found it useful to complete the list in parts—for example, adding twenty or thirty items at a time. If you carry around a notebook or phone, you can also add items when you have a few minutes to spare, for instance, on public transportation or while waiting in line. It can be interesting to see how your lists evolve over time. One of the reasons I like Adams' suggestion of aiming for one hundred items is that it might sound daunting at first, but it is achievable. It doesn't matter if you repeat certain items. In fact, it's useful to think about the significance of these repetitions.

Lists can also be shorter. When I am tired or feel pushed for time, one of my favorite journaling exercises is simply to make a list of things I achieved during the day (a "have done" list), qualities I've felt glad to have (a "have been" list), qualities I'd like to embody tomorrow (a "to be" list), or enjoyable moments that happened during the day.

Even if I begin by struggling to find positive things to write about a stressful and frustrating day, I start small and am soon aware of several, if not many, things I appreciate. Quite often my opinion of a day can change as a result of this exercise, and I end feeling much more at peace with the last twenty-four hours.

Other possible lists include a morning list of things you want to achieve during the day, a bucket list of things you want to do before you die, a list of your favorite words, and a list of things you are most grateful for. You can find several suggestions for lists of one hundred in the journaling prompts at the end of this chapter. The possibilities for types of lists are endless, and they show that journaling doesn't have to be a serious exercise. It can be fun too!

Example List:

Ten Things I Appreciate About Journaling:

1. The freedom

2. The surprises

3. Having a record of things I've done and experienced

4. Getting to know myself

5. Finding out more about the different parts of myself

6. Seeing things from another perspective

7. Being able to let it all out

8. Learning to like all parts of me

9. A fresh notebook

10. That it's just for me

List Suggestions:

- Childhood dreams I remember ...
- One hundred things that make me happy ...
- Places I would like to visit ...
- When I think of *home*, I think of ...
- Twenty ways I can show someone I care ...

29: FRIENDSHIPS

We all have a need for social connection. Sometimes we go into friendships consciously, knowing exactly what we need and want from a friendship, and choose our closest companions using specific criteria.

Sometimes, however, friends are more like people we pick up as we go through life. We might have friends that we tolerate more than appreciate. Our friendship circle might contain people met through school, college, or work, who don't quite meet our needs for connection, acceptance, and closeness, but who we keep around for fear of being lonely or judged.

Whether you think your relationships might fall into the former or latter categories, friendship is a ripe subject for journaling. You can use the following questions as starting points to consider. Try answering them in a stream-of-consciousness fashion, going with whatever comes into your head first and developing from there. Remember, there are no right or wrong answers—this is about your experience of friendship.

- What do you define as *friendship*?
- How do you choose your friendships?
- How do you think your friends perceive you?
- What would you like more of in your friendships?
- What would you like less of in your friendships?

30: A LIST OF PROMPTS

Prompts cover a wide range of journaling topics and can be used for pretty much anything. Similar to springboards, prompts are useful when you sit down to write and then your mind goes blank. Some prompts are fertile ground, and you can go back to them more than once.

So far we've talked about twenty-nine different suggestions for journaling in the previous pages, so here is a list of fifty prompts to get you started:

- A day I really enjoyed
- Something that's troubling me right now
- A description of one of my favorite people
- Something I've always dreamed of doing is …
- When I think of the future, I think about …
- Who am I today?
- Someone from my past who I'd like to see again is …
- A dream that really stayed with me
- If I went back in time and saw myself as a child, I would tell me …
- A list of one hundred things I want

- A list of one hundred things I like about myself
- A list of one hundred things I would do if money and time weren't an issue
- A visualization of my life one year from now
- A description of something I feel very grateful for
- An unsent letter to [choose a recipient]
- A character sketch of my mother
- A character sketch of myself from my mother's point of view
- A character sketch of my father
- A character sketch of myself from my father's point of view
- A list of one hundred things I feel proud of
- A description of something I regret
- A strange incident
- If I were to write a book, I would write about …
- A description of a time when I felt really moved
- Happiness is …
- Love is …
- A character sketch of my ideal partner
- Something I don't like talking about
- A character sketch of my ideal self
- A description of a time I laughed really, really hard
- A list of one hundred things I can do to take care of myself
- A dialogue with my body about food
- A dialogue with my body about my exercise habits
- A dialogue with my body about smoking, alcohol, or another unhealthy activity
- A dialogue with my body about my self-image
- A dialogue with my body about self-acceptance
- A dialogue with a certain part of me about self-care
- A dialogue with my body about accessories and adornments (such as jewelry, clothes, hair coloring, etc.)

- Today I am …
- A time I felt content was …
- A list of one hundred things I want to do during my life
- Something I've never told anyone is …
- When I think about death, I think of …
- When I think about life, I think of …
- A beautiful memory I have is …
- When I think about the idea of having children, I feel …
- Something I've tried in the past that I'd like to try again is …
- Something I would do differently if I had the chance to do it again is …
- What I want to get out of a regular journaling practice
- The most important thing for me to experience in my life is …

PART 3
USING ART FOR JOURNALING

INTRODUCTION

Enlarge your consciousness. If your consciousness is small, you will experience smallness in every department of your life.
—*Robert Pante*

Art has long been considered an effective therapeutic medium, and the process of creating and encouraging creativity can be both revealing and cathartic.

When it comes to journaling, words aren't for everyone. Some people feel more comfortable expressing themselves through the medium of art than they do writing. Even if you enjoy writing, journaling through art can open up new and previously unexplored avenues that lead to expanded awareness and understanding.

You don't have to be an artist to journal using art. The mediums and style you use are completely your decision, and the images you produce don't have to be realistic. Just like written journaling, there is no right or wrong way to journal using art, and your artwork isn't for anyone else to see, evaluate, or judge. It is about your self-expression and what's happening for you internally.

31: CHARACTER PORTRAITS

Several written suggestions in this book refer to the different parts of our personality. I've focused on our internal child, parent, and adult, but different people visualize their different internal voices in a variety of ways. However you view your internal dialogue, it's interesting to develop your image of these characters in more detail.

You can do this by creating a portrait of the character. If you feel more comfortable doing so, you can also describe the character using words.

The portrait can be in any style you wish—from a formal painting to a labeled textbook-style diagram. It can be life-like, abstract, or anything in between. The purpose of this isn't to judge your art skills but to be able to hear and communicate with your internal characters with more clarity.

32: DRAWING YOUR MOOD

This suggestion has several variations, all of which explore expressing emotion through art in different ways. For all of these ideas, you can experiment with creating your image while looking at the page, as well as creating it purely by touch without looking at the page. Remember that these don't have to result in a "picture." Instead they are a way for you to experiment with expressing yourself.

1. Using pens, pencils, paints, or other mediums, create an impression of your mood at this moment. Choose colors, textures, and shapes that represent how you are feeling right now (you can also include words, if it feels right).

2. Using a medium of your choice, create an artistic representation of the mood you would like to feel at this moment, for example, happy, relaxed, excited, etc.

3. Find a piece of music that moves you or that you feel expresses your current mood and draw the sounds. This can also be a helpful way of influencing your moods. Upbeat music can help you feel more positive, while slower, steadier music can help you feel more relaxed.

33: EXPRESSED VISUALIZATION

In Part 2, we looked at written visualizations that involve meditating, then writing down what images, thoughts, and feelings emerge.

An expressed visualization is an art-based version of that exercise and involves expressing what you want for the future through the use of colors, shapes, and images, rather than the use of words.

To create an expressed visualization, start by meditating on a certain area of your life (you can use the Visualization Template in Part 2). Once the meditation has finished, record images and feelings using drawing, colors, paint, collage, or anything else that takes your fancy.

As well as focusing on what you want to be doing within a certain time period, you can also explore what kind of relationships you want to have with people and things.

Ideas for visualizations include:

- How would I like to see and experience my body?

- How would I like to experience and treat my emotions?
- How would I like to experience and treat my partner?

34: MOOD BOARDS

Mood boards are helpful for delving into your unconscious thoughts and feelings, and for inspiring new ideas.

To create a mood board, start with a large piece of crafting card or paper, assorted magazines or newspapers, paints, embellishments, and anything else you want to use. Then focus on a certain topic, for example, what you want to achieve during the next year.

Start looking for colors, images, words, and textures that represent that topic for you. Stick them onto the card in any order, style, or pattern you want. Don't pay too much attention to detail. Just go with the flow.

Mood boards can be completed in one sitting or over a period of weeks or months, as it strikes your fancy. This is a very creative, intuitive exercise. There's very little conscious thought involved, and you might be surprised by the finished product.

35: RELATIONSHIPS AND SUPPORT

This suggestion involves evaluating your current relationships and support system, and comparing your existing network to your ideal.

It provides a visualization of your personal community and can help make clearer how much support you have, as well as those areas of your life in which you could use more. You can include friends, family, acquaintances, colleagues, and anyone else you feel who supports you.

Start by drawing yourself at the center of your page. Then draw each of the closest people in your life in a circle around you. This is your inner circle. Connect a line from you to them, like you're drawing a spider diagram. Create another outer layer to the circle by drawing people you consider friends, but who aren't as close as your inner circle. Keep adding layers to your circle until you have included everyone you want to.

Is there anyone outside the inner circle who you'd like to be closer to in the future or vice versa?

Next, write down the area of your life in which each person gives you the most support. This might be your personal development, relationships, work, practical issues, problem-solving, and so on.

Are there any areas you can identify where you don't feel very supported? If so, what can you do to change that?

36: SELF-PERSPECTIVE

This suggestion explores how we see ourselves and how we view our physical reflections. You will need paper, pencils, and a mirror.

To start, place the mirror at a certain angle, and draw yourself as you see yourself (note: this doesn't have to be realistic; it's about your perception). Try this from as many angles as possible.

Alternatively you can try creating different sketches based on how you perceive yourself in different situations, for example, out with friends, with a significant other, with your family, and at work.

Remember that these images are not a test of your artistic skill and that they can also contain any words or phrases that you feel are relevant.

37: YOU VERSUS THE WORLD

How we see ourselves can differ from how the rest of the world sees us. You might have experienced seeing yourself in a picture, or hearing your voice on a recording, and thinking *I look/sound like that?!*

The differences don't stop with our physical aspects, however. People can often experience us in a very different way than we imagine, yet most of us rarely ask for feedback concerning how our friends and family think and feel about us.

We also tend to keep some parts of ourselves hidden from view, through fear that they are not acceptable or will be judged by others. It can be helpful to look at what we think of ourselves, compared to how we think other people see us.

To start, take a blank sheet of paper and divide the page in half. On the top half, draw yourself how you think others see you. On the bottom half, draw yourself as you think you really are.

Like the other artistic suggestions in this book, your drawings do not have to be realistic. You can use any shapes or colors you like to represent the two halves. What's important is that you find a way of expressing the two perspectives that feels comfortable. Answer these questions:

What do you notice about the differences between the two halves?

Is there anything on the bottom half that you would like to bring more into the top half too?

38: SELF-PORTRAIT

A lot of the suggestions in this section have focused on us as individuals in relation to the rest of the world. This suggestion is similar to the last one, You versus the World, as it explores how we perceive ourselves.

For this last suggestion, create a self-portrait using mixed media. You can use absolutely anything you want, and it's not supposed to be realistic.

Simply visualize you as you see yourself—this can be your physical appearance, your character, or both—and create an impression of what you can see using whatever materials you feel drawn to.

PART 4
OTHER TOOLS

INTRODUCTION

This section of *The Ultimate Guide to Journaling* focuses on what to do with the fruits of your practice. The act of journaling is useful in itself, but the pages, text files, or audio clips we produce are a gold mine of information, waiting to be viewed with a fresh perspective.

In this last part of the book, you'll find information on what I call "retrospecting," looking back on past journaling notes. You'll also find information about dissociation and the inner child—two key concepts that might help you view your journaling from a new angle and deepen your level of self-awareness. I've also included a chapter on language and on how noticing the way we talk about ourselves and others when we journal can help improve the quality of our communication.

Finally I've included a Further Resources section, where you can find more information about books, websites, and software that will help expand your journaling horizons as you continue with your journey. You can also find a live list of these resources here: www.becomingwhoyouare.net/guidetojournalingresources

RETROSPECTING

The art of living lies less in eliminating troubles than in growing with them.
—Bernard Baruch

Why look back?

Although the act of writing down thoughts and feelings in itself can be cathartic, going back and reading over them later can make the experience even more worthwhile and rewarding.

As we read what we've written, we can observe patterns, changes, and similarities. Just as there is no right time or method when journaling, there is no right time or method for retrospecting. Sometimes it can be useful to retrospect weekly, looking back on the writing we've done over the last seven days. Other times it can be more helpful to look at the bigger picture and do a monthly or even yearly retrospect.

Timing

The timing of your retrospect will depend on what you want to get out of it. Regular weekly reviews (for instance, on Sunday nights) can help us evaluate the past week, and work out what our priorities and focus points will be for the week ahead. Alternatively retrospection can be done every month or every quarter. This time period is useful for providing a more long-term review and planning session. These can be instrumental in evaluating visualizations and recognizing whether you have stayed on track or whether you want to set some new goals for the months ahead.

Yearly retrospects can be conducted any time, although birthdays and the start of a New Year can provide useful landmarks. Yearly reviews allow us to see how much has changed in the last twelve months, how far we've come toward achieving our goals, and also lets us speculate where we'd like to be this time next year.

For example, a birthday is the perfect time to make a list of One Hundred Things I Achieved When I Was X Years Old/One Hundred Things I'd Like to Achieve While I'm X Years Old. A prompt for the next year might be "In 2013/14/15, etc., this is the year I will …" The possibilities are endless.

Methods

The type of retrospecting you do depends on what works best for you as an individual. Some people find simply reading and thinking about their previous journaling entries helpful. Alternatively you might want to develop a list of questions you ask yourself every week, month, or year. This could include the best and worst parts of that time, what you are taking into the next week/month/year, and what thoughts have come up for you as you've been reading your past entries.

Just as Parts 2 and 3 provided a variety of ideas for journaling, the suggestions from those sections are useful methods for retrospecting too. Remember, there are no rules. Some of the thoughts that come up when reviewing your journaling can be used as springboards, or perhaps you'd like to do a character sketch of some of the people who have been key figures in your life during this period. You might even want to revisit stepping stones you've already written about to see whether your thoughts and feelings around the topics have changed.

Benefits

The process of retrospecting can help you revisit comfortable and uncomfortable feelings, and you can gain many benefits from taking the time to look back.

Retrospecting can show us where we have gained closure and can bring the things that still aren't resolved to the surface. It can also bring back old feelings and repressed emotions. We might feel old guilt or shame around some of our thoughts, feelings, and behaviors, and even promote a self-attack about our past actions and so-called "negative" thoughts. Many people sometimes feel resistance to retrospecting for this reason (me included). However, as unpleasant as it might be to feel these emotions again, it's a useful signal that there's still some processing to do around the events that provoke these feelings.

Dwelling solely on the past is unhelpful, but returning to what has been with a curious and open mind is a different exercise entirely. It allows us to see how far we've come, to look back on situations and see how we felt then, to have compassion for our past selves, to learn from our mistakes, to relive joy-filled moments, and to compare the memories we hold now to the words we used to describe the events at the time.

THE INNER CHILD AND
DISSOCIATION

Do I contradict myself?
Very well then I contradict myself,
(I am large, I contain multitudes.)
—Walt Whitman

Although journaling can help us explore and address any number of concerns, events, or issues, I want to introduce two ideas in particular. The first is the concept of the inner child and how journaling can help us create a more productive inner dialogue. The second is the idea of dissociation and how journaling can help us access plus express emotions that might be buried in the past.

The Inner Child and Other Characters

The inner child is the part or parts of ourselves stuck in the past. These parts still seek the love and acceptance we wanted but didn't always get from our caregivers, and they carry that search into adulthood, seeking solace in romantic relationships, workaholism, and other sometimes self-abusive behaviors. You don't necessarily have to have suffered "serious" abuse as a child to have these parts. We're all hurt, angered, and humiliated at times, and very few children are allowed to freely express these emotions without being dismissed or punished.

As we grow up, we develop three main internal characters. These are the inner child, the parent, and the adult. When certain feelings are triggered or we experience certain situations, one of these characters can become dominant over the others. We might also find that two of the characters conflict, and we literally start a fight with ourselves. An example of this is when we feel intensely upset about something, while thinking, *This is ridiculous. I shouldn't be crying*. One internal part is working on a "feeling" level and expressing hurt, while the other is working on a "thinking" level and dismissing the validity of the feeling.

If you've ever experienced a flood of emotions, like an overwhelming feeling of anger, humiliation, or something similar, that's the inner child. I'm not necessarily talking about intense emotions; for me, overwhelming emotions are those I feel I simply must act on and do something about, or emotions I can't contain. Whenever I've felt an overwhelming emotion, I can trace it back to the inner child. And this doesn't just mean "negative" (or uncomfortable) emotions either. It includes floods of happiness, joy, serenity, and peace too.

My inner child was one of the scariest parts I uncovered through journaling and therapy. There was lots of hurt, pain, and neglect, as well as ongoing attacks from my inner parent to add to that. Dealing with the thoughts and the feelings of my inner child has been one of the harder and darker periods of my own journaling. My inner child and my inner parent still have problems getting along at times, but using a third adult voice to mediate between the two parts has greatly improved my internal dialogue. I discuss the topics of inner children, inner parents, and creating a more peaceful relationship with ourselves in my book *The Power of Self-Kindness: How to Transform Your Relationship with Your Inner Critic*.

Exploring the world of the inner child might bring up a lot of uncomfortable feelings, and I would recommend having a therapist or trusted friend on hand who you can talk to if needed. It's hard, but it's worth it. By exploring your internal characters, not only do you connect to vitally important parts of yourself but you get to really live; to feel more, to experience more, and to do so in the moment. Journaling isn't always a barrel of laughs. I've felt intensely uncomfortable about some of the things I've written in the past—but I've discovered new parts of myself I never knew existed, and these discoveries have made my life infinitely richer.

Dissociation

Dissociation is an epidemic in our society. It's a coping mechanism and a survival technique that kicks in when parts of us think bad consequences would result from expressing our feelings or our genuine reaction to a situation. These bad consequences might be punishment or rejection from others, or a fear of feeling overwhelming negative emotions within ourselves.

A simplified definition of dissociation is: when we cut off or repress our feelings, partially or entirely, reducing the amount of empathy we can feel from others or ourselves.

For example, I tend to dissociate in the presence of aggressive people, because, deep down, they absolutely terrify me. When I'm not aware of my terror, I don't feel as uncomfortable; however, I'm also less likely to be able to empathize with my feelings and take action, such as removing myself from a potentially volatile situation.

It's an effective coping mechanism, because it's a useful way of dealing with traumatic situations. If we're trapped in a burning building, it's a good idea to switch to the nonfeeling "thought" part of our brain rather than the "feeling" part, as the "thought" part will be looking for the exit, while the "feeling" part will be panicking. It's probably obvious which part is more likely to help us survive. Like the inner child, dissociation doesn't just include "negative" emotions. It's perfectly possible to dissociate from "positive" ones too.

It can be helpful to think of emotions like the images on a heart monitor. A healthy emotional experience has spikes and troughs as the heart beats and as we go through the ups and downs of life. A dissociated person's conscious emotional experience is like a flatline. It's steady, consistent, and, in extreme cases, pretty lifeless.

Childhood abuse and neglect can prime adults for dissociation. If you were verbally, physically, emotionally, or sexually abused as a child, you most likely had to dissociate certain feelings, including pain, anger, and fear, in order to survive. Even if you didn't suffer overt abuse, many children grow up realizing that certain emotions aren't acceptable. As this reaction is learned early on, it's unconscious and, therefore, difficult to unlearn in adulthood without self-work and introspection. Part of us still thinks it's healthy. When we are under attack, perceived or real, we don't want to express our most vulnerable side, so we erect a steel wall of impassable blankness and dissociate instead.

Although dissociation is designed for our self-protection, it has its dark side. Dissociation is not just unhealthy, it's dangerous. As I said above, it can cause the inability to feel empathy for ourselves or others. In extreme cases of dissociation, this lack of empathy might lead us to put ourselves into situations that are bad for our mental or physical health. It might lead us to behave in a detrimental way toward others.

Journaling helps bust dissociation and bust it good. That's because the emotions we dissociate from don't go anywhere. They're still there, hiding in split-off parts of ourselves, just looking for an opportunity to get out. Repressing feelings is like playing a never-ending game of Whac-A-Mole. You push one down, and another pops up; you act quickly to push that one down and, oops! There goes another one.

They might seem like different entities, but dissociation, repression, and the uncovering of the inner child can be intrinsically linked, as sometimes the feelings from which we want to dissociate are those that come from the inner child.

Allowing all thoughts and feelings to come through, to have a voice, and to be expressed will reduce the level of dissociation you experience. It won't happen overnight—it might take weeks, months, or even years. But the more time you spend letting buried emotions through, the less you'll be reacting to the past, and the more you'll be able to see present situations clearly, responding to what's happening and to how you feel right here, right now.

LANGUAGE

Your own words are the bricks and mortar of the dreams you want to realize... The words you choose and use establish the life you experience.
—Sonia Choquette

The language we use in our journaling can reveal a lot about our feelings, including our level of empathy and acceptance toward ourselves and others.

It can be helpful to notice the kind of language we use to refer to the different parts of our personality and other people in our lives. This isn't to stop ourselves from saying certain things—I'm against self-censorship in journaling—but simply so that we become more aware.

When revisiting the language you use in your journaling, you're looking for two types of words:

1. Judgmental words or phrases, such as *bad*, *wrong*, *great*, etc., which are all moral or value judgments we make about ourselves and others.

2. Feeling words or phrases, such as *hurt, angry, happy*, etc., which are all about how we experienced a person, event, or situation on an emotional level.

A few years ago I read *Nonviolent Communication* (Puddle Dancer Press, 2003), or *NVC* as I will use herein, by Marshall Rosenberg. This book blew my mind. It's had a huge impact on the way I think about myself and how I communicate with others.

In a nutshell, there are three main components to *NVC*. The first is self-empathy; the second is empathy for others; and the third is honest, authentic communication.

NVC emphasizes the universal feelings and needs that humans experience. Rosenberg says that everything we do is an attempt to get these needs met. Examples of universal needs include acceptance, empathy, closeness, growth, and self-expression. When we have conflicts with other people, or conflicts within ourselves, there is a conflict of needs and a miscommunication about those needs. This miscommunication often involves judgmental and manipulative language (what Rosenberg calls Jackal language) that leads the person on the receiving end to feel guilty, ashamed, or afraid. We might get into an argument with someone and label them or call them names, or we might experience our inner critic telling us we're not good enough, lazy, fat, and so on.

When we can empathize with our own needs (met or unmet), empathize with the needs of others, and communicate that empathy in a way that the other person understands (what Rosenberg calls Giraffe language), we are communicating openly and giving ourselves the best chance possible of meeting our needs.

So, when you look back at your journaling, consider the kind of language you're using. Is there more Jackal than Giraffe? If so, that's understandable. We live in a Jackal world, and judgmental statements and assumptions are, ironically, tolerated far more than talking openly and honestly about our feelings. This language, however, is not one of compassion, and it doesn't enable us to meet our needs, nor help others meet theirs.

A helpful template for thinking about how to communicate our feelings and needs without judgment is:

When [insert event or behavior here],

I feel [an emotion].

I need [a specific nonblaming request].

For example:

When you told me your assumption about why I didn't take out the trash, *I felt* hurt and angry. *I need* you to ask me what my reasons are for doing something, rather than act on your assumptions.

Can you talk about yourself and the different parts of your personality with more compassion?

Is there miscommunication about needs between different parts of you?

If so, how can you understand the needs of those individual parts better and help them both get their needs met?

To learn more about the concept and practice of nonviolent communication, visit The Center for Nonviolent Communication's website (cnvc.org). There you will find information about the center's work, as well as lists of feelings and needs that are helpful reference tools. I have my copy stuck to my wall, and it's been invaluable for developing my Giraffe vocabulary.

WHAT NEXT?

Thank you for reading *The Ultimate Guide to Journaling*! I hope you found this book helpful and that it's inspired you to think about your journaling practice in a new way.

If you haven't already, please consider leaving a brief review. It doesn't have to be long; 1-2 sentences is just fine. Reviews are incredibly valuable for indie authors and I appreciate each and every one, so thank you!

This book is part of a wider range of content I publish through my website, Becoming Who You Are. VisitBecoming Who You Are (www.becomingwhoyouare.net) to find practical psychology-based articles and resources on creating a full and meaningful life with greater courage, compassion, and creativity. As a quick reminder, you can get your free video class on starting (or restarting) your journaling practice by going to http://journaling.becomingwhoyouare. net/book and entering your email. When you register, you'll also get more free workbooks, video classes and more tools for personal growth in the Becoming Who You Are Library (I will never, ever share your email and you are free to unsubscribe at any time).

I'd love to hear your thoughts about this book, so please email me at **hannah@becomingwhoyouare.net** with any questions, suggestions, or feedback.

Happy journaling!

FURTHER RESOURCES

It is what we do in the present to help shape the future that counts.
—Graham Gordon Ramsey and Holly Barlow Sweet

I hope you've enjoyed this ebook, and found the ideas and suggestions useful for your own journaling practice.

Here is a list of resources I've found helpful. Some of them have influenced this book, and all will help you delve deeper into the world of journaling.

For a living list of resources relevant to this book, please visit www.becomingwhoyouare.net/guidetojournalingresources

You can also get your free video class on starting (or restarting) a journaling practice here.

Books

Journal to the Self - Kathleen Adams

A friendly and encouraging guide to journaling containing twenty-two suggestions for developing your journaling practice.

Getting Things Done - David Allen

A time-management system that helps you complete tasks, make decisions, and manage life more consciously.

The Courage to Heal - Ellen Bass and Laura Davis

A workbook for survivors of sexual abuse.

The Well-Being Journal - Lucia Capacchione

A guide to visual journaling, focusing on our relationships with our body and well-being.

Self-Therapy - Jay Earley, PhD

An accessible introduction to Internal Family Systems Therapy and the idea of internal parts.

Creative Visualization - Shakti Gawain

A handbook on how to use visualizations to evaluate our current beliefs and perceptions, and to make conscious our wishes, dreams, and ambitions for the future.

All About Me - Philipp Keel

A book of prompts that explores your life experiences so far.

Becoming the Way We Are - Pamela Levin

A workbook for exploring how events and experiences in different stages of childhood affect our relationships with ourselves and others today.

The Woman's Comfort Book - Jennifer Louden

A beautiful book full of suggestions for self-nurture and relaxation.

A Creative Guide to Exploring Your Life - Graham Gordon Ramsey and Holly Barlow Sweet

An inspiring exploration of how art and photography can help us explore different issues and topics.

Nonviolent Communication - Marshall Rosenberg

An examination and explanation of how to express our feelings and needs, and enjoy peaceful communication with others.

Internal Family Systems Therapy - Richard Schwartz

An explanation of Schwartz's internal family systems theory and the idea of internal parts. This is the first book published on the subject and is more academic than Jay Earley's book.

Private Myths - Anthony Stevens

An exploration of dreams and dreaming.

The Mindful Way through Depression - Mark Williams, John Teasdale, Zindel Segal, and Jon Kabat-Zinn

An excellent book that is suitable for everyone. It provides tips and techniques for developing mindfulness in our everyday lives and staying in touch with our bodies.

Websites, Software, and e-Courses

4 Weeks of Self-Knowledge: http://www.becomingwhoyouare.net/classes/4-weeks-of-self-knowledge/

A four-week sentence-completion course that kick-starts your self-knowledge in ten minutes a day.

750 words: http://www.750words.com

A fun way to develop a regular journaling practice, with quirky badges and "awards" to incentivize daily writing.

Macjournal by Mariner Software: http://www.marinersoftware.com/products/macjournal

Journaling software for Windows and Mac that helps you organize your journaling notes digitally and keep them private.

Day One: http://dayoneapp.com/

My favourite journaling software that allows you to sync between multiple devices and now comes with encryption

Sentence Completion: http://www.nathanielbranden.-com/exercises/sentence-completion-i

A thirty-week sentence-completion program based on Nathaniel Branden's book The Six Pillars of Self-Esteem.

Penzu: http://www.penzu.com

A private online space you can keep your journaling notes, pictures, and clippings. Smartphone and tablet users can also download apps and sync their notes across several devices.

Progoff Intensive Journal Program: http://www.intensive-journal.org

Offering courses, training, and workbooks, the Progoff Intensive Journal Program helps you explore all areas of your life through the act of journaling.

ALSO BY HANNAH BRAIME

The Year of You: 365 Journal Writing Prompts for Creative Self-Discovery

Are you ready to go on a journey?

The Year of You is an invitation to discover more about yourself, become more conscious about what you want, and create a rich and fulfilling life through one journaling prompt a day. This book provides you with 365 structured journaling prompts to explore the most important areas of your life, from identity, health, and relationships, to money, career, and the future. Whether you're new to journaling or have enjoyed a reflective writing practice for some time, this book provides a wealth of inspiration that will deepen your understanding and awareness of what makes you who you are.

The Year of You for Mothers

Do you want to reconnect with your sense of who you are and what matters most to you? Could you benefit from a daily dose of reflection and self-connection?

The Year of You for Mothers is your opportunity to spend a few minutes with yourself each day. As well as reflecting on your parenting experience, you'll also maintain (or regain) that important connection with the areas of your life that can get pushed aside by the daily whirlwind of parenting.

Inside, you'll find 365 daily journaling prompts that will make you think about a specific aspect of your life and your parenting experience, including identity, purpose and meaning, community, money, health, and more.

From Coping to Thriving: How to Turn Self-Care Into a Way of Life

From Coping to Thriving **is a comprehensive guide to making self-care part of your everyday life.** With a balance between practical suggestions, coaching-style questions and psychological groundwork, this book is designed to give you the self-knowledge and awareness you need to start making self-care an integral part of your life. Not only does *The Ultimate Guide to Journaling* contain hundreds of useful self-care tips and ideas, it will also take you deeper into related topics like habit-formation, coping strategies, dealing with resistance to self-care and more.

The Power of Self-Kindness

In *The Power of Self-Kindness: How to Transform Your Relationship With Your Inner Critic*, you'll discover a radical approach to healing your relationship with your inner critic and yourself, one based on understanding, self-acceptance and self-compassion.

Whether you've been struggling with your inner critic for a long time or are at the beginning of your self-kindness journey, this book offers a range of approaches and suggestions you can use to mend the most important relationship in your life: the one with yourself.

ABOUT THE AUTHOR

Hannah Braime writes about journaling, self-care, and creativity. She is the author of four other books, including *The Year of You: 365 Journal Writing Prompts for Creative Self-Discovery* and *From Coping to Thriving: How to Turn Self-Care Into a Way of Life*. She also shares practical psychology-based articles and resources on creating a full and meaningful life with greater courage, compassion, and authenticity at www. becomingwhoyouare.net.

Stay in touch to hear more about future books:
www.becomingwhoyouare.net
hannah@becomingwhoyouare.net

Made in the USA
Monee, IL
22 December 2022